More than MAGNIFIERS

Grades 6–9

Skills
Observing, Comparing, Measuring, Graphing

Concepts
Lenses, Images, Focal Length, Magnifiers, Cameras,
Telescopes, Projectors, Field of View

Themes
Systems & Interactions, Models & Simulations,
Structure, Stability, Patterns of Change,
Scale, Energy, Matter

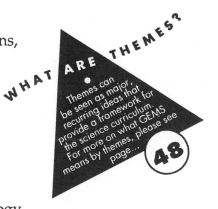

WHAT ARE THEMES?

Themes can be seen as major, recurring ideas that provide a framework for the science curriculum. For more on what GEMS means by themes, please see page...

48

Nature of Science and Mathematics
Scientific Community, Interdisciplinary,
Cooperative Efforts,
Changing Nature of Facts & Theories,
Theory-Based and Testable,
Real-Life Applications, Science and Technology

Time
Four 30- to 50-minute sessions

Cary I. Sneider
and
Alan Gould

LHS GEMS

Great Explorations in Math and Science (GEMS)
Lawrence Hall of Science
University of California at Berkeley

Illustrations
Carol Bevilacqua

Photographs
Richard Hoyt

Lawrence Hall of Science, University of California, Berkeley, CA 94720. Chairman: Glenn T. Seaborg; Director: Marian C. Diamond

Publication was made possible by grants from the A.W. Mellon Foundation and the Carnegie Corporation of New York. This support does not imply responsibility for statements or views expressed in publications of the GEMS program. GEMS also gratefully acknowledges the contribution of word processing equipment from Apple Computer, Inc. Under a grant from the National Science Foundation, GEMS Leader's Workshops have been held across the country. For further information on GEMS leadership opportunities, please contact GEMS at the address and phone number below.

International Standard Book Number: 0-912511-62-1

COMMENTS WELCOME

Great Explorations in Math and Science (GEMS) is an ongoing curriculum development project. GEMS guides are revised periodically, to incorporate teacher comments and new approaches. We welcome your criticisms, suggestions, helpful hints, and any anecdotes about your experience presenting GEMS activities. Your suggestions will be reviewed each time a GEMS guide is revised. Please send your comments to: GEMS Revisions, c/o Lawrence Hall of Science, University of California, Berkeley, CA 94720. The phone number is (415) 642-7771.

Great Explorations in Math and Science (GEMS) Program

The Lawrence Hall of Science (LHS) is a public science center on the University of California at Berkeley campus. LHS offers a full program of activities for the public, including workshops and classes, exhibits, films, lectures, and special events. LHS is also a center for teacher education and curriculum research and development.

Over the years, LHS staff have developed a multitude of activities, assembly programs, classes, and interactive exhibits. These programs have proven to be successful at the Hall and should be useful to schools, other science centers, museums, and community groups. A number of these guided-discovery activities have been published under the Great Explorations in Math and Science (GEMS) title, after an extensive refinement process that includes classroom testing of trial versions, modifications to ensure the use of easy-to-obtain materials, and carefully written and edited step-by-step instructions and background information to allow presentation by teachers without special background in mathematics or science.

Staff

Glenn T. Seaborg, Principal Investigator
Jacqueline Barber, Director
Cary Sneider, Curriculum Specialist
Katharine Barrett, John Erickson, Rosita Fabian, Kimi Hosoume, Laura Lowell, Linda Lipner, Carolyn Willard, Staff Development Specialists
Jan M. Goodman, Mathematics Consultant
Cynthia Ashley, Administrative Coordinator
Gabriela Solomon, Distribution Coordinator
Lisa Haderlie Baker, Art Director
Carol Bevilacqua and Lisa Klofkorn, Designers
Lincoln Bergman and Kay Fairwell, Editors

Contributing Authors

Leigh Agler
Jeremy Ahouse
Jacqueline Barber
Katharine Barrett
Lincoln Bergman
Marion E. Buegler
David Buller
Linda De Lucchi
Jean Echols

Alan Gould
Cheryll Hawthorne
Sue Jagoda
Jefferey Kaufmann
Robert C. Knott
Larry Malone
Cary I. Sneider
Elizabeth Stage
Jennifer Meux White

Reviewers

We would like to thank the following educators who reviewed, tested, or coordinated the reviewing of this series of GEMS materials in manuscript form. Their critical comments and recommendations contributed significantly to these GEMS publications. Their participation does not necessarily imply endorsement of the GEMS program.

ARIZONA

David P. Anderson
Royal Palm Junior High School, Phoenix

Joanne Anger
John Jacobs Elementary School, Phoenix

Cheri Balkenbush
Shaw Butte Elementary School, Phoenix

Flo-Ann Barwick Campbell
Mountain Sky Junior High School, Phoenix

Sandra Caldwell
Lakeview Elementary School, Phoenix

Richard Clark*
Washington School District, Phoenix

Kathy Culbertson
Moon Mountain Elementary School, Phoenix

Don Diller
Sunnyslope Elementary School, Phoenix

Barbara G. Elliot
Tumbleweed Elementary School, Phoenix

Joseph M. Farrier
Desert Foothills Junior High School, Phoenix

Mary Anne French
Moon Mountain Elementary School, Phoenix

Leo H. Hamlet
Desert View Elementary School, Phoenix

Elaine Hardt
Sunnyslope Elementary School, Phoenix

Walter Carroll Hart
Desert View Elementary School, Phoenix

Tim Huff
Sunnyslope Elementary School, Phoenix

Stephen H. Kleinz
Desert Foothills Junior High School, Phoenix

Alison Lamborghini
Orangewood Elementary School, Phoenix

Karen Lee
Moon Mountain Elementary School, Phoenix

George Lewis
Sweetwater Elementary School, Phoenix

Tom Lutz
Palo Verde Junior High School, Phoenix

Midori Mits
Sunset Elementary School, Phoenix

Brenda Pierce
Cholla Junior High School, Phoenix

Sue Poe
Palo Verde Junior High School, Phoenix

Robert C. Rose
Sweetwater Elementary School, Phoenix

Liz Sandberg
Desert Foothills Junior High School, Phoenix

Jacque Sniffen
Chaparral Elementary School, Phoenix

Rebecca Staley
John Jacobs Elementary School, Phoenix

Sandra Stanley
Manzanita Elementary School, Phoenix

Chris Starr
Sunset Elementary School, Phoenix

Karen R. Stock
Tumbleweed Elementary School, Phoenix

Charri L. Strong
Mountain Sky Junior High School, Phoenix

Shirley Vojtko
Cholla Junior High School, Phoenix

K. Dollar Wroughton
John Jacobs Elementary School, Phoenix

CALIFORNIA

Carolyn R. Adams
Washington Primary School, Berkeley

Judith Adler*
Walnut Heights Elementary School, Walnut Creek

Gretchen P. Anderson
Buena Vista Elementary School, Walnut Creek

Beverly Braxton
Columbus Intermediate School, Berkeley

Dorothy Brown
Cave Elementary School, Vallejo

Christa Buckingham
Seven Hills Intermediate School, Walnut Creek

Elizabeth Burch
Sleepy Hollow Elementary School, Orinda

Katharine V. Chapple
Walnut Heights Elementary School, Walnut Creek

Linda Clar
Walnut Heights Elementary School, Walnut Creek

Gail E. Clarke
The Dorris-Eaton School, Walnut Creek

Sara J. Danielson
Albany Middle School, Albany

Robin Davis
Albany Middle School, Albany

Margaret Dreyfus
Walnut Heights Elementary School, Walnut Creek

Jose Franco
Columbus Intermediate School, Berkeley

Elaine Gallaher
Sleepy Hollow Elementary School, Orinda

Ann Gilbert
Columbus Intermediate School, Berkeley

Gretchen Gillfillan
Sleepy Hollow Elementary School, Orinda

Brenda S.K. Goo
Cave Elementary School, Vallejo

Beverly Kroske Grunder
Indian Valley Elementary School, Walnut Creek

Kenneth M. Guthrie
Walnut Creek Intermediate School, Walnut Creek

Joan Hedges
Walnut Heights Elementary School, Walnut Creek

Corrine Howard
Washington Elementary School, Berkeley

Janet Kay Howard
Sleepy Hollow Elementary School, Orinda

Gail Isserman
Murwood Elementary School, Walnut Creek

Carol Jensen
Columbus Intermediate School, Berkeley

Dave Johnson
Cave Elementary School, Vallejo

Kathy Jones
Cave Elementary School, Vallejo

Dayle Kerstad*
Cave Elementary School, Vallejo

Diane Knickerbocker
Indian Valley Elementary School, Walnut Creek

Joan P. Kunz
Walnut Heights Elementary School, Walnut Creek

Randy Lam
Los Cerros Intermediate School, Danville

Philip R. Loggins
Sleepy Hollow Elementary School, Orinda

Jack McFarland
Albany Middle School, Albany

Betty Maddox
Walnut Heights Elementary School, Walnut Creek

Chiyomi Masuda
Columbus Intermediate School, Berkeley

Katy Miles
Albany Middle School, Albany

Lin Morehouse*
Sleepy Hollow Elementary Schoool, Orinda

Marv Moss
Sleepy Hollow Elementary School, Orinda

Tina L. Neivelt
Cave Elementary School, Vallejo

Neil Nelson
Cave Elementary School, Vallejo

Joyce Noakes
Valle Verde Elementary School, Walnut Creek

Jill Norris
Sleepy Hollow Elementary School, Orinda

Janet Obata
Albany Middle School, Albany

Patrick Pase
Los Cerros Intermediate School, Danville

Geraldine Piglowski
Cave Elementary School, Vallejo

Susan Power
Albany Middle School, Albany

Louise Rasmussen
Albany Middle School, Albany

Jan Rayder
Columbus Intermediate School, Berkeley

Masha Rosenthal
Sleepy Hollow Elementary School, Orinda

Carol Rutherford
Cave Elementary School, Vallejo

Jim Salak
Cave Elementary School, Vallejo

Constance M. Schulte
Seven Hills Intermediate School, Walnut Creek

Robert Shogren*
Albany Middle School, Albany

Kay L. Sorg*
Albany Middle School, Albany

Marc Tatar
University of California Gifted Program, Berkeley

Mary E. Welte
Sleepy Hollow Elementary School, Orinda

Carol Whitmore-Waldron
Cave Elementary School, Vallejo

Vernola J. Williams
Albany Middle School, Albany

Carolyn Willard*
Columbus Intermediate School, Berkeley

Mary Yonekawa
The Dorris-Eaton School, Walnut Creek

KENTUCKY

Joyce M. Anderson
Carrithers Middle School, Louisville

Susan H. Baker
Museum of History and Science, Louisville

Carol Earle Black
Highland Middle School, Louisville

April B. Bond
Rangeland Elementary School, Louisville

Sue M. Brown
Newburg Middle School, Louisville

Donna Ross Butler
Carrithers Middle School, Louisville

Stacey Cade
Sacred Heart Model School, Louisville

Sister Catherine, O.S.U.
Sacred Heart Model School, Louisville

Judith Kelley Dolt
Gavin H. Cochran Elementary School,
Louisville

Elizabeth Dudley
Carrithers Middle School, Louisville

Jeanne Flowers
Sacred Heart Model School, Louisville

Karen Fowler
Carrithers Middle School, Louisville

Laura Hansen
Sacred Heart Model School, Louisville

Sandy Hill-Binkley
Museum of History and Science, Louisville

Deborah M. Hornback
Museum of History and Science, Louisville

Patricia A. Hulak
Newburg Middle School, Louisville

Rose Isetti
Museum of History and Science, Louisville

Mary Ann M. Kent
Sacred Heart Model School, Louisville

James D. Kramer
Gavin H. Cochran Elementary School,
Louisville

Sheneda Little
Gavin H. Cochran Elementary School,
Louisville

Brenda W. Logan
Newburg Middle School, Louisville

Amy S. Lowen*
Museum of History and Science, Louisville

Mary Louise Marshall
Breckinridge Elementary School, Louisville

Theresa H. Mattei*
Museum of History and Science, Louisville

Judy Reibel
Highland Middle School, Louisville

Pamela R. Record
Highland Middle School, Louisville

Margie Reed
Carrithers Middle School, Louisville

Donna Rice
Carrithers Middle School, Louisville

Ken Rosenbaum
Jefferson County Public Schools, Louisville

Edna Schoenbaechler
Museum of History and Science, Louisville

Karen Schoenbaechler
Museum of History and Science, Louisville

Deborah G. Semenick
Breckinridge Elementary School, Louisville

Dr. William McLean Sudduth*
Museum of History and Science, Louisville

Rhonda H. Swart
Carrithers Middle School, Louisville

Arlene S. Tabor
Gavin H. Cochran Elementary School,
Louisville

Carla M. Taylor
Museum of History and Science, Louisville

Carol A. Trussell
Rangeland Elementary School, Louisville

Janet W. Varon
Newburg Middle School, Louisville

MICHIGAN

Glen Blinn
Harper Creek High School, Battle Creek

Douglas M. Bollone
Kelloggsville Junior High School, Wyoming

Sharon Christensen*
Delton-Kellogg Middle School, Delton

Ruther M. Conner
Parchment Middle School, Kalamazoo

Stirling Fenner
Gull Lake Middle School, Hickory Corners

Dr. Alonzo Hannaford*
Western Michigan University, Kalamazoo

Barbara Hannaford
The Gagie School, Kalamazoo

Duane Hornbeck
St. Joseph Elementary School, Kalamazoo

Mary M. Howard
The Gagie School, Kalamazoo

Diane Hartman Larsen
Plainwell Middle School, Plainwell

Miriam Hughes
Parchment Middle School, Kalamazoo

Dr. Phillip T. Larsen*
Western Michigan University, Kalamazoo

David M. McDill
Harper Creek High School, Battle Creek

Sue J. Molter
Dowagiac Union High School, Dowagiac

Julie Northrop
South Junior High School, Kalamazoo

Judith O'Brien
Dowagiac Union High School, Dowagiac

Rebecca Penney
Harper Creek High School, Battle Creek

Susan C. Popp
Riverside Elementary School, Constantine

Brenda Potts
Riverside Elementary School, Constantine

Karen Prater
St. Joseph Elementary School, Kalamazoo

Joel Schuitema
Woodland Elementary School, Portage

Pete Vunovich
Harper Creek Junior High School, Battle
Creek

Beverly E. Wrubel
Woodland Elementary School, Portage

NEW YORK

Frances P. Bargamian
Trinity Elementary School, New Rochelle

Barbara Carter
Jefferson Elementary School, New Rochelle

Ann C. Faude
Heathcote Elementary School, Scarsdale

Steven T. Frantz
Heathcote Elementary School, Scarsdale

Alice A. Gaskin
Edgewood Elementary School, Scarsdale

Harriet Glick
Ward Elementary School, New Rochelle

Richard Golden*
Barnard School, New Rochelle

Seymour Golden
Albert Leonard Junior High School, New
Rochelle

Don Grant
Isaac E. Young Junior High School, New
Rochelle

Marybeth Greco
Heathcote Elementary School, Scarsdale

Peter C. Haupt
Fox Meadow Elementary School, Scarsdale

Tema Kaufman
Edgewood Elementary School, Scarsdale

Donna MacCrae
Webster Magnet Elementary School, New
Rochelle

Dorothy T. McElroy
Edgewood Elementary School, Scarsdale

Mary Jane Motl
Greenacres Elementary School, Scarsdale

Tom Mullen
Jefferson Elementary School, New Rochelle

Robert Nebens
Ward Elementary School, New Rochelle

Eileen L. Paolicelli
Ward Elementary School, New Rochelle

Donna Pentaleri
Heathcote Elementary School, Scarsdale

Dr. John V. Pozzi*
City School District of New Rochelle, New
Rochelle

John J. Russo
Ward Elementary School, New Rochelle

Bruce H. Seiden
Webster Magnet Elementary School, New
Rochelle

David B. Selleck
Albert Leonard Junior High School, New
Rochelle

Lovelle Stancarone
Trinity Elementary School, New Rochelle

Tina Sudak
Ward Elementary School, New Rochelle

Julia Taibi
Davis Elementary School, New Rochelle

Kathy Vajda
Webster Magnet Elementary School, New
Rochelle

Charles B. Yochim
Davis Elementary School, New Rochelle

Bruce D. Zeller
Isaac E. Young Junior High School, New
Rochelle

DENMARK

Dr. Erik W. Thulstrup
Royal Danish School of Educational Studies,
Copenhagen

*Trial test coordinators

Contents

Acknowledgments

The activities in this unit were developed by Budd Wentz and Alan Gould in the 1970s. Alan Friedman pointed out the educational importance of using pairs of lenses with the same diameters but different focal lengths. The authors adapted the various activities to create a classroom unit. Jacqueline Barber integrated the comments of teachers and reviewers to help produce the first edition, and Alan Gould was instrumental in making significant revisions in the second edition of this GEMS teacher's guide.

Introduction

Children love to play with magnifiers. They soon find out that some lenses magnify more than others. Through daily experience they learn that lenses are also used in a wide variety of optical instruments, from cameras to eyeglasses. This unit provides students with the exciting chance to discover how the same kinds of lenses they've played with as magnifiers can be combined to construct many other optical devices.

In this series of activities, your students find out how lenses are used in magnifiers, simple cameras, telescopes, and slide projectors. They learn that lenses have properties that can be measured, and that some lenses are better for specific purposes than others. As the students explore the properties of lenses, they also have many opportunities to develop the important science skills of manipulating laboratory materials, observing, comparing, measuring, and solving problems creatively.

Presenting these activities does not require a detailed knowledge of the physics of light or optics. "Behind the Scenes," beginning on page 37, contains background information on the properties and functions of the lenses in the four devices constructed in this unit. If you read the background information and try out each activity yourself before presenting it to your students, you should be well prepared to teach the unit.

Summary Outlines are provided to help you guide your students through the unit in an organized way. Student data sheets appear immediately following the session in which they are needed. Removable copies of student data sheets are included at the end of the booklet.

It's important to plan ahead. This unit requires a class set of two different lenses. You can use lenses you already have on hand, or purchase lenses as suggested in the "Getting Ready" section on page 4 of this guide. Allow at least a month for your order to be filled. Acquiring a set of lenses for your students is worth the time and cost, as lenses have many uses throughout the science curriculum.

Younger students may find the concepts in this unit to be challenging. Older students may at first consider the more elementary concepts as a review, but they will in turn be challenged by the more complex ideas that build from one activity to the next. Both the background information in "Behind the Scenes," and the "Going Further" ideas suggested at the end of each activity can assist you in designing a unit that is appropriate for even the most advanced students.

As your students achieve the objectives of each activity, they progressively acquire a concrete understanding of the properties that enable lenses to create useful and fascinating effects. This practical knowledge forms a valuable foundation for more abstract concepts presented in high school physics courses. At the same time, your students gain familiarity with optical instruments they encounter or interact with every day, from cameras and projectors to the lenses in their eyes.

Have your students explore *More Than Magnifiers* and watch their understanding of lenses magnify!

Time Frame

Teacher Preparation	60 minutes
Activity 1: Magnifiers	30–45 minutes
Activity 2: Cameras	30–45 minutes
Activity 3: Telescopes	30–45 minutes
Activity 4: Projectors	30–45 minutes

What You Need (for all activities)

For the class:

- ☑ 1 one-gallon clear glass jug or jar
- ☑ a sheet of newspaper
- ☐ 1 inexpensive portable lamp with no shade
- ☑ 1 25′ extension cord
- ☐ 1 40–75 watt red bulb
- ☑ 1 roll of masking tape
- ☐ 2 8½″ x 11″ sheets of lightweight tracing paper
- ☑ chalk and chalkboard
- ☐ (*Optional*) a camera, a commercial lens-type telescope, and a slide projector

For each team of two or three students:

- ☐ 1 lens, 40–100 mm focal length
- ☐ 1 lens, 80–300 mm focal length (The second lens of the pair must have a focal length at least twice as long as the first. See "Purchase Lenses" in "Getting Ready" on page 4.)
- ☐ 3 8-oz. styrofoam cups
- ☐ 1 color slide
- ☑ 1 flashlight (See "Acquire Slides and Flashlights" in "Getting Ready" on page 7.)
- ☑ 1 sheet of white paper
- ☑ 1 pen or crayon for writing on styrofoam cups

For each student:

- ☐ 1 "Magnifiers" data sheet
- ☐ 1 "Cameras" data sheet
- ☐ 1 "Telescopes" data sheet
- ☐ 1 "Projectors" data sheet

(Masters included, pages 13, 20, 28, 36.)

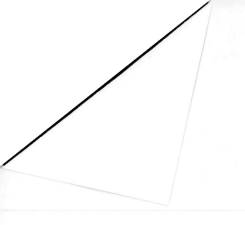

Getting Ready

Before You Begin the Unit:

1. Purchase lenses. Well in advance of when you plan to teach this unit, you will need to order a pair of lenses for every three students in your class. One lens of the pair must have a focal length at least twice as long as the other. The lenses should be at least 1" in diameter so they form bright images. Either plastic or glass lenses will work for these activities. It is ideal for the two lenses to have the same diameter but different focal lengths, so that students can see that it is curvature, not diameter, that makes the difference in how much the lens magnifies objects, or the size of the images it projects.

Class sets of plastic lenses with different focal lengths but equal diameters may be purchased inexpensively from the Lawrence Hall of Science GEMS Project. For more information, phone (415) 642-7771. Lenses can also be purchased through optical supply houses, such as the Edmund Scientific Company in Barrington, New Jersey. Lenses purchased for this unit can be used in other parts of the science curriculum, as magnifiers and in other activities that explore optics.

If you have a supply of lenses, but do not know their focal lengths, project an image of the sun or some other distant light source onto a piece of paper or other surface. To determine the focal length of the lens, measure the distance between the lens and the focused image of the light source.

DISTANT SUN

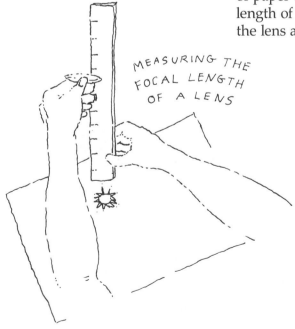

MEASURING THE FOCAL LENGTH OF A LENS

2. Mount lenses by taping them to the bottoms of styrofoam cups with transparent tape. You may wish to have several students help with this task. If the lenses you are using are of different diameters, make sure they are mounted so their centers are at the same height. Do not disassemble the cup and lens apparatus until you have completed the unit.

3. Duplicate data sheets. For each of your students, make one copy of each of the four data sheets: "Magnifiers," "Cameras," "Telescopes," and "Projectors." (Masters on pages 13, 20, 28, 36.)

4. Try out each activity yourself. This experience will help you demonstrate the procedures to your class, and help you anticipate problems your students may encounter and questions they may ask.

5. Read the background information included in "Behind the Scenes," beginning on page 37.

6. Arrange student work areas. For all activities, arrange tables or desks so that teams of three students can work together. For Activities 2, 3, and 4, place the lamp with a bare red bulb in the center of the room and arrange the work areas around the periphery of the room so each group is situated at least five feet from the lamp and can see it clearly.

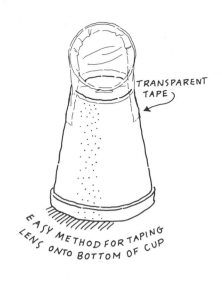

TRANSPARENT TAPE

EASY METHOD FOR TAPING LENS ONTO BOTTOM OF CUP

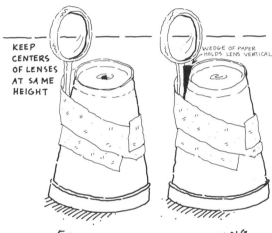

KEEP CENTERS OF LENSES AT SAME HEIGHT

WEDGE OF PAPER HOLDS LENS VERTICAL

EASY METHOD FOR TAPING LENS WITH HANDLES ONTO CUP

Before Activity 1:

Fill a jug or jar with water. Hold it in front of a sheet of newspaper. The picture or writing will appear "stretched out" in width when viewed through the jug. Set these aside for use as a demonstration at the end of the class.

Before Activities 2, 3, and 4:

1. Prepare to darken the room. If your room cannot be darkened, consider using the auditorium or multi-purpose room. Ideally students should work at tables. However, if necessary, the "Cameras," and "Projectors" activities will also work on the floor. A dark room is more important for the "Projectors" activity than for the previous activities. Close curtains or tape cloth over windows so that when you turn out the overhead light, the only light sources will be the red lamp in the middle of the room, and the flashlights used by each team.

2. Set up the lamp. Place the lamp with a 40–75 watt red bulb in the center of the room. Any type of lamp will do, but you must remove the shade, exposing the bare bulb. The red bulb provides a good bright source of light without impairing the students' abilities to see clearly in a dimly-lit room. The height of the bulb must be the same as the height of the lenses when they are taped to their cup mounts on top of the tables or desks. This can be done by standing the lamp on a desk, clipping it to a chair, or hanging it from the ceiling.

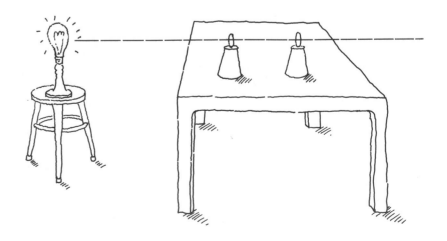

Before Activity 4:

1. Acquire slides and flashlights. Sometime before you present the "Projectors" activity, collect slides by sending a note home to parents asking for color slides that do not need to be returned. It is important that the picture be in focus. Having students bring in flashlights from home is also a good way to acquire the number of flashlights that are needed.

2. Prepare flashlights by "sandwiching" a disk of tracing paper between the reflector and the clear plastic disk. You may wish to have your students do this.

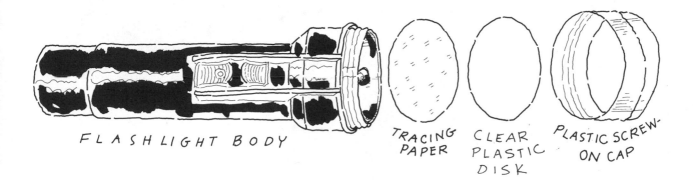

FLASHLIGHT BODY

TRACING PAPER

CLEAR PLASTIC DISK

PLASTIC SCREW-ON CAP

Activity 1: Magnifiers

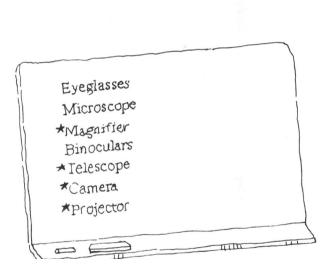

Overview

In this activity, the students draw pictures of their fingers as viewed through two different magnifiers. They compare the two magnifiers, and find that one makes things appear larger than the other. They see that a jug of water can also act as a magnifier, and discover that the property that enables a lens to magnify is the curvature of its surface.

This activity provides your students with an important prerequisite for the entire unit. The main objective is for the students to understand how the curvature of a lens determines both its magnifying power and its field of view. If you want to provide your students with more activities on this subject, see the suggestions in "Going Further" on page 12. The first three of these activities could be used to extend the lesson for students who finish early. The other two activities require additional equipment.

Introducing Magnifiers

1. Ask your students to name things that use *lenses* [eyeglasses, telescopes, microscopes, etc.]. Write their ideas on the chalkboard.

2. Tell the students that in this unit they will conduct a series of activities to help them understand four different instruments that use lenses. Make a star next to "magnifier," "camera," "telescope," and "projector," if these are listed on the chalkboard. If not, add them to the list.

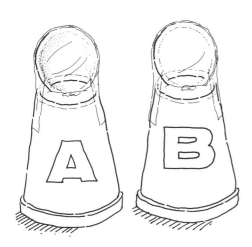

3. Explain that today they will investigate the magnifying properties of lenses. You may wish to define *magnifier* as a lens used to make things look bigger, and ask the following questions:

- How do magnifiers differ from each other?

- Raise your hand if you have observed that some lenses magnify more than others.

- Why do you think some lenses magnify more than others?

Accept all of the students' responses and add that they will find out the answers to these and other questions about magnifiers through this activity.

4. **Divide the class into teams of two or three students. Distribute one of each lens to each team of students.** Ask the students to feel the lenses and describe how they are different. Have them label the lens that is curved more "A" and the lens that is curved less "B" by writing on the cups.

5. Tell the students that their challenge is to draw what they see with each lens, and to determine which lens makes things appear bigger. Demonstrate how to hold the lens, and how to use it to magnify the back of your hand, sleeve, watch, or some other object.

6. Explain that what your students see through the lens when they look at an object is called an *image* of that object. Add that usually when an image is first seen through a lens, the image has blurry edges, or is what is called *"out of focus."* If the distance from a lens to an object is set just right, the image edges are clear and sharp, and the image is *"in focus."*

Investigating Magnifiers

1. Read and demonstrate the instructions on the data sheet.

2. Distribute one data sheet to each student, and let the teams of students work together on the steps outlined on their data sheets. Circulate among the groups and provide assistance as needed.

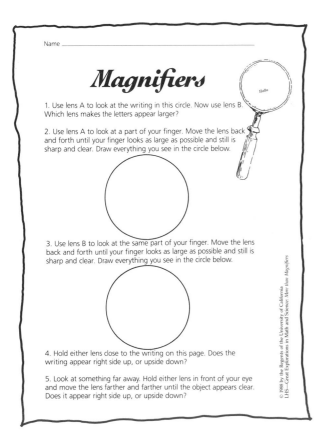

Name _____

Magnifiers

1. Use lens A to look at the writing in this circle. Now use lens B. Which lens makes the letters appear larger?

2. Use lens A to look at a part of your finger. Move the lens back and forth until your finger looks as large as possible and still is sharp and clear. Draw everything you see in the circle below.

3. Use lens B to look at the same part of your finger. Move the lens back and forth until your finger looks as large as possible and still is sharp and clear. Draw everything you see in the circle below.

4. Hold either lens close to the writing on this page. Does the writing appear right side up, or upside down?

5. Look at something far away. Hold either lens in front of your eye and move the lens farther and farther until the object appears clear. Does it appear right side up, or upside down?

© 1988 by the Regents of the University of California
LHS—Great Explorations in Math and Science: *More than Magnifiers*

3. Some groups will finish earlier than others. Let these groups explore the lenses on their own. When all groups have finished, it is important to collect the lenses. Otherwise, the students will continue to experiment, and be distracted from the discussion.

Discussing How Magnifiers Work

1. Take a poll of the students' answers to the first question: "Which lens makes things appear larger, lens A or lens B?" If there are differences of opinion, have groups who disagree discuss their experiments for a few minutes to see if they can come to agreement. If the conclusion is still unclear, redistribute the lenses and have the students redo the experiment.

2. Explain that the reason that lens A magnifies more is because it is more steeply curved than lens B.

3. Demonstrate how a clear object that is curved can magnify things by taking out the jug of water and showing how a picture or writing placed behind it appears to stretch out sideways. You can carry the jug around the room to show all of the students, or invite them to come up to a central table for a closer view.

4. Draw a diagram (as shown in the margin) showing how the lens "fools our eyes" into thinking that the light comes from a much wider object, by bending the light. The lens magnifies an object the same way that the jug does, but rather than just stretching out the object sideways, it magnifies the object in height as well as width. This is because a lens is curved in all directions, like a part of a ball.

5. Define the *magnifying power* of a lens as the number of times bigger it can make an object appear. The greater the curvature of a lens, the greater its magnifying power.

6. Invite students to share their observations, made in steps 2 and 3 on the data sheet, of the appearance of their fingers under a magnifying lens. Define the area viewed through a magnifier as the *field of view.* Ask if a lens that magnifies more shows a smaller or larger field of view. [Smaller.]

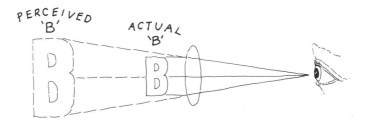

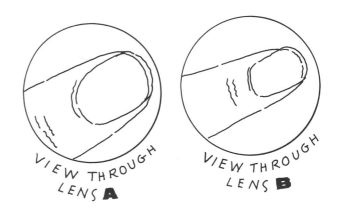

7. End the activity by asking the students for their answers to questions 4 and 5 on the data sheet, in which they look at objects very close to the lens, and far away, and see if things appear right side up or upside down. [They will find that when the lens is used to magnify objects that are close, the image is right side up. When used to look at something far away, the image is upside down and smaller.] Tell the students that they will learn why the image of distant objects is upside down during the next activity, when they explore cameras.

Going Further

1. Have your students use the two lenses to explore and draw other things: various types of cloth, a torn edge of paper, the hair on their arms. Studying the same things with two different magnifiers will allow students to draw more conclusions about the differences between the lenses.

2. Encourage your students to explore the "flip point"—the point at which objects observed through a lens flip from right side up to upside down. Have them determine whether the "flip point" for lens A or for lens B is closer to their eyes. The "flip point" is actually the focal point that your students learn about in the next activity on cameras.

3. Have your students experiment with the lenses in eyeglasses to see if they magnify when held close to an object. Most eyeglass lenses are negative lenses—they diverge rather than converge light, so they make things appear smaller rather than bigger.

4. Bring in a collection of other lenses and have your students investigate their magnifying properties and fields of view.

5. Have your students make a water drop magnifier by placing a piece of waxed paper (or clear plastic) over a newspaper square and putting a drop of water on the waxed paper (or clear plastic). Why does the newsprint appear larger? [The dome-shaped drop of water acts as a lens.]

5. Have your students make a water drop magnifier by placing a piece of waxed paper over a news paper

Magnifiers

Hello

1. Use lens A to look at the writing in this circle. Now use lens B. Which lens makes the letters appear larger?

2. Use lens A to look at a part of your finger. Move the lens back and forth until your finger looks as large as possible and still is sharp and clear. Draw everything you see in the circle below.

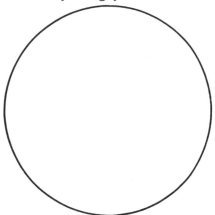

3. Use lens B to look at the same part of your finger. Move the lens back and forth until your finger looks as large as possible and still is sharp and clear. Draw everything you see in the circle below.

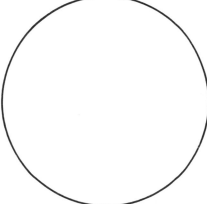

4. Hold either lens close to the writing on this page. Does the writing appear right side up, or upside down?

5. Look at something far away. Hold either lens in front of your eye and move the lens farther and farther until the object appears clear. Does it appear right side up, or upside down?

Activity 2: Cameras

Overview

In this activity, the students project images of a light bulb onto a piece of paper, just as a camera lens projects images onto film. They measure the distance between the lenses and the images they project, the *image distance*. They find that a lens with a less steep curvature projects a larger image than a lens with a steeper curvature, even though the more curved lens is a more powerful magnifier. The students discover that a lens projects an upside-down image when it is held far enough away from an object.

"Going Further" on page 19 contains suggestions for extending the activity by having students practice projecting images, make "movie" cameras, delve into the photographic concept of f-stop, and graph the measured focal length in relation to the object distance.

Introducing Cameras

1. Review with your students what they learned about magnifying lenses in the last activity:

- Which is a more powerful magnifer, lens A or lens B? [Lens A.]

- What characteristic of lens A makes it a more powerful magnifier? [It is more steeply curved.]

- How does a lens make something appear bigger? [It bends the light, fooling us into thinking it comes from a larger object.]

2. Tell the students that today they will use the same lenses they used as magnifiers to make *cameras.* Find out what your students know about cameras, and set the stage for the activity by asking questions, such as:

- What are some of the differences between cameras?

- Comparing a telephoto lens with a wide-angle lens, which magnifies more? Which has a larger field of view?

- How are telephoto camera lenses different from wide-angle camera lenses?

- **Which lens do you think would have a greater curvature, a telephoto lens or a wide-angle lens?**

Accept all responses and explain that during the activity they will find out whether or not their answers to these and other questions are correct.

3. Hand out the "Cameras" data sheets. Read and demonstrate the instructions to your students before handing out the lenses. You do not need to form images on the paper, but rather show how the lenses and paper should be placed. Emphasize that the images should be sharply focused before the distance between the lens and the paper screen is measured. Tell the students to observe whether the image of the bulb on the screen is right side up or upside down.

Investigating Camera Lenses

1. Hand out the two lenses and a blank sheet of paper to each pair of students. Remind them of the challenge: to measure the image distance of each lens. Turn on the lamp in the center of the room and turn off the room lights. Tell the students to follow the steps outlined on their data sheets. Circulate among the groups and help students as needed.

2. Challenge students who finish early to experiment with the lenses on their own. When all groups have finished, collect the lenses. Turn on the room lights, and turn off the lamp.

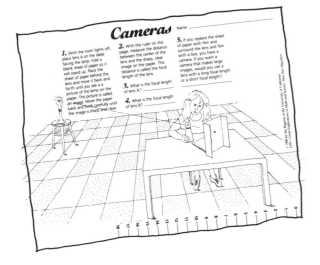

Discussing How Cameras Work

1. Poll the tems for their measurements of the image distances of lens A and lens B. The students will find that lens A has a shorter image distance than lens B. Tell them that Lens A is called a *short focus lens* and lens B is called a *long focus lens*.

2. Ask which lens projected the biggest image. If there are disagreements, have teams talk together to resolve differences of opinion. If necessary, distribute lenses and have the students experiment until they agree. The students may be surprised to discover that lens B makes a larger image than lens A, since they previously found that lens A is a more powerful magnifier.

3. Draw the diagram shown on this page on the chalkboard to explain why the most powerful magnifier makes a smaller image when used as a camera, and why the image it makes is upside down:

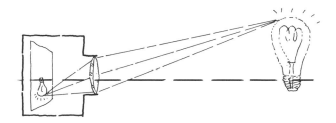

The axis is the line that is perpendicular to the lens.

    a. Ask where the light in the picture comes from. [The bulb.] Explain that the light from the bulb spreads out in all directions. Some of it hits the lens.

    b. Ask your students if they remember from the previous activity what a lens does to light. [It bends the light.]

    c. Trace three sample light rays from the top of the bulb showing that all rays from one point on the bulb that strike the lens are bent and meet at one point on the image. If the light comes from above the axis of the lens, the image focal point is below the axis. Light from below the axis of the lens focuses on the image above the axis. That is why the image is upside down.

d. Ask the students if they remember what they would see if the object is very close to the lens. [It appears magnified and right side up.] Redraw the diagram of a magnifier from the previous activity, which shows that if the object is very close to the lens, it is magnified and appears right side up. If **the object is far enough from the lens, it projects an upside-down image of the object.**

4. Summarize by saying: when used as a magnifier, the lens is held very close to the object we are observing, and we see the object right side up. When as a camera, the lens is usually a long way from the object and is projected onto film or paper upside down.

5. Add that cameras that make large images on film use very long focus lenses called *telephoto lenses*. Cameras that make small images but take in a large area use very short focus lenses called *wide-angle lenses*.

6. Point out that a real camera is set up in the same way, but it projects the image onto film instead of paper, and the entire apparatus is enclosed in a box. You may want to ask why a camera needs to be enclosed. [To protect the film from light.]

7. If you have a camera to demonstrate, point out the lens and open the back of the camera to show where the film is placed. In some cameras it is possible to open the shutter for a time exposure. If you can do that, open the camera back and place a sheet of white paper where the film goes. Point the camera at a window, and you will see an image of the window projected onto the paper.

8. End the activity by asking the students if they have any questions, or if they have had experiences with cameras that they would like to share with the class.

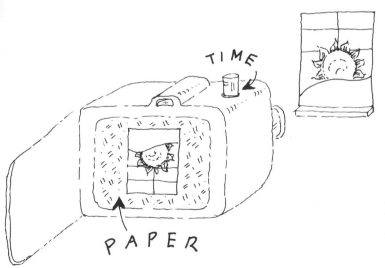

Going Further

1. Challenge your students to use lenses to project images of the classroom lights onto the table tops. If they get stumped, tell them to imagine that the ceiling light is the red light bulb and the table top is the paper screen.

2. Have your students make "movie cameras" by projecting a moving image onto the wall. Tell one student to stand with the lenses along the wall furthest from the classroom windows, while another student moves her arms in front of the window. The student next to the wall can project a moving image on the wall of his partner. The students can compare the moving images formed by each of the two lenses.

3. Present some of the information described in "Behind the Scenes" about photographic concepts, such as *f-stop*.

4. Ask a photographer to bring in a camera with different lenses, and to explain to your students how she uses them. You can also have students bring cameras from home and list similarities and differences.

5. Find the *focal length*. Have your students make a data sheet with two columns, labeled "Object Distance," and "Image Distance." Give each group a meter stick in addition to the lenses and paper screens used in this activity. Tell the students to place Lens A various distances from the light bulb (0.5 meters, 1 meter, 2 meters, etc.) and to measure the image distance of the lens at each position. Have them graph their results using "Object Distance" along the vertical axis and "Image Distance" along the horizontal axis. They will observe that as the lens is moved farther and farther from the object, the image distance decreases to a certain minimum value, and then will not decrease any more, no matter how far the lens is placed from the object. This limit is called the *focal length* of the lens.

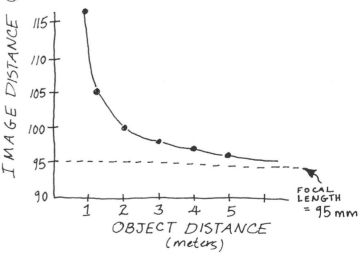

OBJECT DISTANCE (meters)	IMAGE DISTANCE (millimeters)
.05	117
1	105
2	100
3	98
4	97
5	97

FOCAL LENGTH = 95 mm

Cameras

Name _____

1. With the room lights off, place lens A on the table facing the lamp. Fold a blank sheet of paper so it will stand up. Place the sheet of paper behind the lens and move it back and forth until you see a picture of the lamp on the paper. This picture is called an **image.** Move the paper back and forth carefully until the image is sharp and clear.

2. With the ruler on this page, measure the distance between the center of the lens and the sharp, clear image on the paper. This distance is called the **image distance.**

3. What is the image distance of Lens A? _____

4. What is the image distance of Lens B? _____

5. If you replace the sheet of paper with film and surround the lens and file with a box, you have a camera. If you want a camera that makes large images, would you use a lens with a long image distance or a short image distance? _____

Activity 3: Telescopes

Overview

A short focus lens and long focus lens are used together in this activity to make a telescope. The students discover that they can make a more powerful telescope if they use the long focus lens in front, as an *objective lens*, and the short focus lens in back, as the *eyepiece*. Reversing the lenses makes things appear smaller, but gives a wider field of view. The students find out that the objective lens projects an image, just like a camera lens, and the eyepiece makes that image appear larger, just like a magnifier.

"Going Further" suggestions include looking at a distant book or object, making a telescope that provides right-side-up images, using cardboard tubes to make a telescope like Galileo made, and visiting an observatory.

Introducing Telescopes

1. Review with your students what they learned about magnifying lenses and cameras in the last two activities:

- Which is a more powerful magnifier, lens A or lens B? [Lens A, the short focus lens.]

- What does a camera lens do? [It projects an image onto film.]

- Which projects a larger image when used as a camera, lens A or lens B? [Lens B, the long focus lens.]

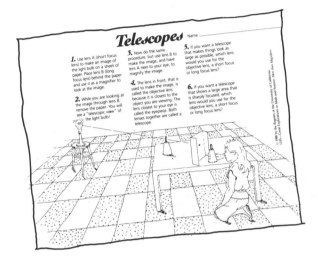

Telescopes
Name _____

1. Use lens A (short focus lens) to make an image of the light bulb on a sheet of paper. Place lens B (long focus lens) behind the paper and use it as a magnifier to look at the image.

2. While you are looking at the image through lens B, remove the paper. You will see a "telescopic view" of the light bulb!

3. Now do the same procedure, but use lens B to make the image, and have lens A next to your eye, to magnify the image.

4. The lens in front, that is used to make the image, is called the objective lens because it is closest to the object you are viewing. The lens closest to your eye is called the eyepiece. Both lenses together are called a telescope.

5. If you want a telescope that makes things look as large as possible, which lens would you use for the objective lens, a short focus or long focus lens?

6. If you want a telescope that shows a large area that is sharply focused, which lens would you use for the objective lens, a short focus or long focus lens?

© 1988 by the Regents of the University of California
LHS—Good Explorations in Math and Science: More Than Magnifiers

2. Tell the class that today they will use the two lenses to make *telescopes*. Ask your students several questions about telescopes:

- What are telescopes used for?

- How do lenses in telescopes alter your vision?

- How are telescopes different from binoculars?

Accept all responses and explain that they will find out the answers to these and other questions through this activity.

3. Distribute the "Telescopes" data sheets. Read and demonstrate the instructions to your students. First show how to project an image onto paper, and then observe the image, using the other lens as a magnifier. Give your students the hint that in order to see the "telescopic view" of the light bulb, their head must be in a line with the two lenses and the light bulb.

4. Remind the students that their challenge is to determine which placement makes a more powerful telescope, having the *short focus lens* (lens A) in front, or having the *long focus lens* (lens B) in front, and which makes a telescope with a wider field of view.

Investigating Telescope Lenses

1. Turn on the lamp and turn out the room lights. Make sure the light bulb is at the same level as the mounted lenses when placed on desks or tables. Distribute the lenses and assist your students as needed to see a telescopic view of the light bulb.

2. When all students have succeeded in seeing a telescopic view of the light bulb with lens A in front, remind them that the challenge is to switch the lenses and see the view with lens B in front (*objective lens*) and lens A as the magnifier (*eyepiece*). Then they should decide which arrangement makes a more powerful telescope, and which makes a telescope with a wider field of view.

3. When the teams finish their experiments, turn on the lights and collect the equipment.

Discussing How Telescopes Work

1. Poll the groups to see which lens arrangement creates a telescope that makes things appear as large as possible. [The long focus lens in front as the objective lens, and the short focus lens next to the eye as the eyepiece lens.] Which arrangement provides the widest field of view? [The short focus lens as the objective lens, and the long focus lens as the eyepiece.]

2. Draw the diagrams on this page on the chalkboard to explain how a telescope works as follows:

    a. Ask the students where the light comes from. [The bulb.]

    b. Ask what the objective lens does to the light. [It forms an image in the air, just like a camera lens forms an image on film.]

    c. Ask what the eyepiece does. [It magnifies the image like a hand magnifier, so it appears bigger.]

    d. You may wish to add that in most telescopes the objective lens is mounted at the end of a long tube. The eyepiece is attached to another tube that can slide in and out of the longer tube to focus the image.

3. Ask the students if the view through their telescopes was right side up or upside down. [Upside down.] Ask them to explain why. [Like a camera, the objective lens projects an image that is upside down. The eyepiece is a magnifier, and does not invert the image.]

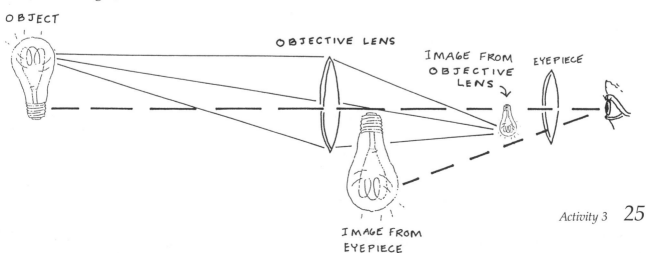

OBJECT

OBJECTIVE LENS

IMAGE FROM OBJECTIVE LENS

EYEPIECE

IMAGE FROM EYEPIECE

4. Ask the students to look at the black pupil in each other's eyes and estimate its size. Explain that all of the light we see must pass through that tiny pupil, since the surrounding iris and white part (sclera) block light. The main purpose of the objective lens in a telescope is to collect light from a much larger area and "funnel" it into a small, bright image. The main purpose of the eyepiece is to magnify that tiny image so we can see fine details. The two lenses acting together make things that are far away appear **bigger** and **brighter**. Both qualities are important for a powerful telescope. The power of a telescope to make objects appear bigger is called *magnifying power*. The power of a telescope to make faint things appear brighter is called *light gathering power*.

5. Ask the class why a commercial telescope has tubes. One reason is to shield the lenses from stray light. In addition, the lenses mounted on the ends of two sliding tubes enable the viewer to keep the lenses aligned and make focusing easier.]

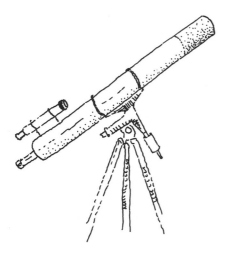

6. (*Optional*) End the activity by showing the students a commercial lens-type telescope if one is available. Ask the students to point out the objective lens and the eyepiece. Take the telescope outdoors, focus on some distant object, and invite the students to form a line to look through the telescope, one at a time. Each student should have the opportunity to focus the telescope until he sees a sharp image.

7. If you do not have a telescope for demonstration, ask the students to raise their hands if they have ever looked through one. Ask individuals to share their experiences with the rest of the class.

8. Explain that *binoculars* are actually two telescopes mounted side by side. Looking through a "telescope" with each eye creates the effect of seeing in three dimensions.

Going Further

1. Have your students use their telescopes to look at distant objects. Ask them to see how far away they can read the (upside down) letters in a book, using their telescopes. [It is best to prop up the book rather than hold it, so the book remains perfectly still.] Your students can make "secret message" words or pictures, tape them upside down on a wall and challenge their classmates on the opposite side of the room to read the message with their telescope lenses.

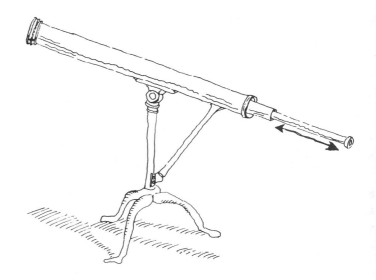

2. Challenge your students to make a telescope that can see things right side up. [This requires three lenses.]

3. Locate sets of sliding cardboard tubes, and have your students tape the pairs of lenses to opposite ends of the tubes to form telescopes like those made and used by Galileo to see the mountains of the moon. Two identical tubes (such as paper towel cores or mailing tubes) can be made into sliding tubes by slitting one of them lengthwise and sliding it over the other one:

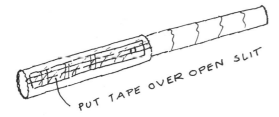

PUT TAPE OVER OPEN SLIT

4. Call a university astronomy department to find out if there is an observatory with a large telescope located nearby. Schedule a field trip to visit it, or invite an astronomer to speak with your students about her work. Local amateur astronomers may be willing to come to your school to demonstrate different kinds of telescopes.

Telescopes

Name _____

1. Use lens A (short focus lens) to make an image of the light bulb on a sheet of paper. Place lens B (long focus lens) behind the paper and use it as a magnifier to look at the image.

2. While you are looking at the image through lens B, remove the paper. You will see a "telescopic view" of the light bulb!

3. Now do the same procedure, but use lens B to make the image, and have lens A next to your eye, to magnify the image.

4. The lens in front, that is used to make the image, is called the **objective** lens because it is closest to the object you are viewing. The lens closest to your eye is called the **eyepiece.** Both lenses together are called a **telescope.**

5. If you want a telescope that makes things look as large as possible, which lens would you use for the objective lens, a short focus or long focus lens? _____

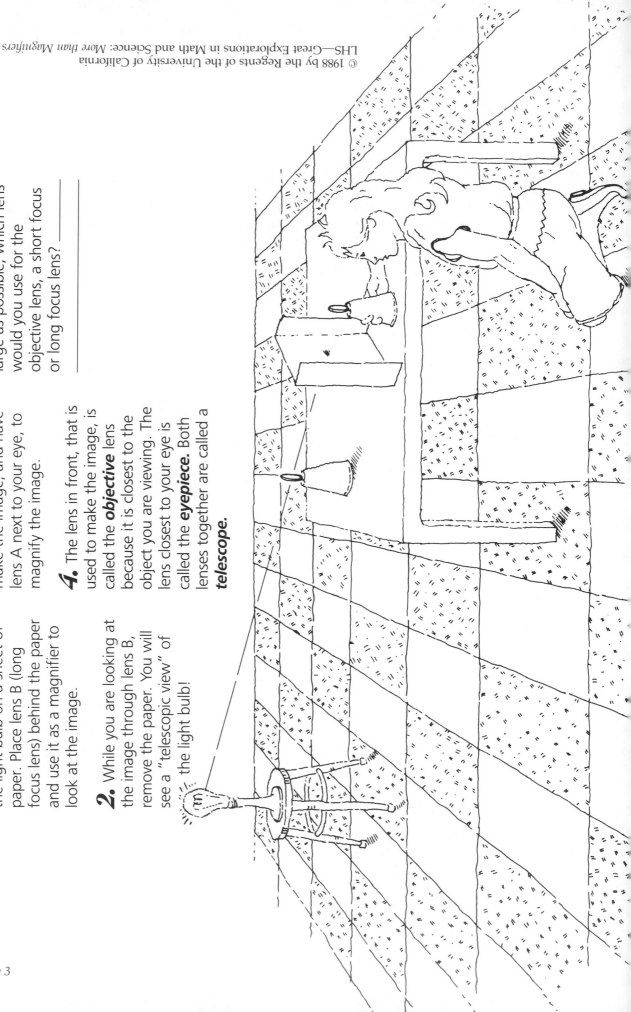

Activity 4: Projectors

Overview

In this activity, your students make table-top slide projectors using a flashlight, slide, and lens. They find that the short focus lens projects a larger image than the long focus lens. They learn that a slide projector is like a camera in reverse: instead of projecting a small image of a distant object, a projector forms a large distant image of a small object (the slide).

Introducing Projectors

1. Review with your students what they learned about telescope lenses in the last activity:

- What is an objective lens? [The front lens in a telescope, closest to the object.]

- What is an eyepiece? [The back lens in a telescope, closest to the eye.]

- Which is a more powerful magnifier, the short focus lens or the long focus lens? [The short focus lens.]

- Which projects a larger image, the short focus lens or the long focus lens? [The long focus lens.]

- If you want a telescope that magnifies as much as possible, which lens is the best one to use as the objective lens? [The long focus lens.] Which is best for the eyepiece? [The short focus lens.]

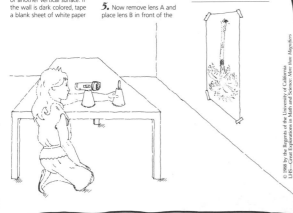

Projectors

In order to make a table-top slide projector that makes as large an image as possible, which lens would you use, a long focus or short focus lens? Follow these steps to find out!

1. Tape the flashlight to the bottom of a cup, making sure that you can turn it on or off.

2. Turn the slide upside down, and tape it to the end of the flashlight.

3. Position the flashlight on a table or desk, about 1.5 meters away from the wall or another vertical surface. If the wall is dark colored, tape a blank sheet of white paper

to the wall, at the same height as the flashlight.

4. Point the flashlight with slide attached toward the wall. Place lens A in front of the slide. Slowly move the lens away from the slide and toward the wall until you see a sharply focused image of the slide projected onto the wall.

5. Now remove lens A and place lens B in front of the

slide. You will have to move the lens quite a distance toward the wall before it will focus. If you cannot focus an image at all, move the flashlight with slide further from the wall and try again.

6. Which lens projects a larger image, the long focus lens or the short focus lens?

2. Find out what your students know about *slide projectors*, asking questions such as the following:

- Do you put slides in right side up or upside down?

- What function does a lens have in a slide projector?

- What is the difference between a long-throw lens and a short-throw lens?

- Would you use a long or short focus lens to "throw" the image of a slide a long distance?

3. Hand out the "Projectors" data sheets. Read and demonstrate the instructions to your students. (You do not need to project an image, just show how the materials are to be placed.)

4. Ask the students to predict which lens will project a larger image of the slide. Tell them that their challenge is to test their predictions.

Investigating Projector Lenses

1. Distribute the pair of lenses, a flashlight, a styrofoam cup, an 8″ strip of masking tape, a white sheet of paper, and one color slide to each pair of students.

2. When the students have taped their flashlights and slides in place, turn off the room lights and turn on the red lamp for general room lighting. (The red light will allow the students to see what they are doing, but not interfere with viewing the image on paper.) Circulate among the students and help as needed.

3. When the students complete the steps on their data sheets, collect all materials except for the data sheets.

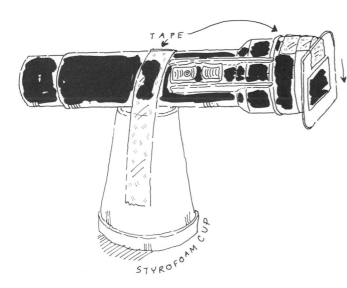

TAPE

STYROFOAM CUP

© 1988 by the Regents of the University of California
LHS—*Great Explorations in Math and Science: More than Magnifiers*

Discussing How Projectors Work

1. Poll the teams for their answers. The students may be surprised to find that the short focus lens projects a larger image, since the long focus lens projected a larger image in both the camera and telescope activities.

2. Explain why the short focus lens projects a larger image by drawing the diagrams on this page on the chalkboard. Explain the findings as follows:

   a. A projector is very much like a backwards camera. The object is small and the image is very large. What is the object here? [The slide.]

   b. Ask the students why they think the image from a projector is so large. [Since the image is very far away it has a chance to spread out and become very large.]

   c. Ask the students why they think the short focus lens projects a larger image. [Because it is curved more, it bends light more, and the light spreads out more, forming a larger image. If the students are confused about situation is different in a camera, follow the light rays backward to see why the shorter focus lens forms a smaller image in a camera.]

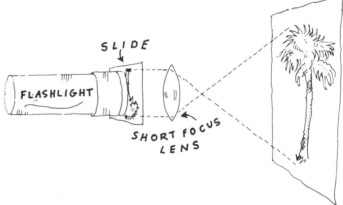

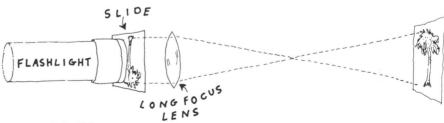

3. (*Optional*) Demonstrate how a commercial slide projector works:

   a. Show how the slide is put in upside down.

   b. Turn the projector on and project an image.

   c. Focus the image onto a screen or the wall and point out how the lens is moved toward and away from the slide to focus the image.

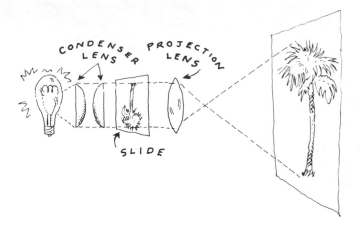

CONDENSER LENS PROJECTION LENS

SLIDE

d. Move the projector closer to the screen and focus it again. Ask your students if the image is larger or smaller.

e. Turn off the slide projector. Open up the top, showing your students the lamp, condenser lenses that make the light parallel as it passes through the slide, and (if possible) the slide and projection lens.

4. Explain what is meant by *long throw* and *short throw* lenses. The lenses in slide projectors may be changed to suit the size of room in which the projector is used. Short throw lenses are used when the slide projector must be close to the screen. Long throw lenses are used when the projector must be a long way from the screen. Ask the students, "Which do you think has a shorter focus, a long throw or a short throw lens? [Short throw lenses have a shorter focus than long throw lenses.]

5. Conclude this activity with some general questions that will help the students conceptualize the relationships between the four optical devices that they studied:

a. Can the same lenses be used to make magnifiers, cameras, telescopes, and projectors? [Yes.]

b. What are the important differences between lenses? [The amount of curvature, image distance, and focal length. You may also want to mention differences in lens diameter and in the materials from which lenses are made.]

c. How does a telescope combine two different functions of lenses? [The objective lens gathers light and forms an image, and the eyepiece magnifies that image.]

d. How are projectors and cameras alike and different? [A camera forms a small image of something far away. A projector forms a large image of something close to the lens. So, a projector is like a backwards camera.]

6. Allow some time for your students to ask questions of their own, or to express their ideas about other optical devices that may have occurred to them during the unit.

Going Further

1. Challenge your students to make a projector using two lenses. How do two lenses affect the image?

2. Knowledge gained through these activities is sufficient to enable your students to design and build a simple slide projector by mounting a flashlight, slide, and lens in a box. The lens can be mounted in a cardboard tube for easier focusing.

3. Have your students study the human eye. Many people are surprised to learn that the eye lens projects an upside-down image onto the back of the eye, on an area called the retina. After the image is transmitted via the optic nerve, the brain turns the image right side up. Your students can learn about eyes by reading about human anatomy, researching the use of eyeglasses and contact lenses, or by dissecting a cow's eye.

NORMAL VISION

RETINA

EYE LENS

The End

Projectors

In order to make a table-top slide projector that makes as large an image as possible, which lens would you use, a long focus or short focus lens? Follow these steps to find out!

1. Tape the flashlight to the bottom of a cup, making sure that you can turn it on or off.

2. Turn the slide upside down, and tape it to the end of the flashlight.

3. Position the flashlight on a table or desk, about 1.5 meters away from the wall or another vertical surface. If the wall is dark colored, tape a blank sheet of white paper to the wall, at the same height as the flashlight.

4. Point the flashlight with slide attached toward the wall. Place lens A in front of the slide. Slowly move the lens away from the slide and toward the wall until you see a sharply focused image of the slide projected onto the wall.

5. Now remove lens A and place lens B in front of the slide. You will have to move the lens quite a distance toward the wall before it will focus. If you cannot focus an image at all, move the flashlight with slide further from the wall and try again.

6. Which lens projects a larger image, the long focus lens or the short focus lens?

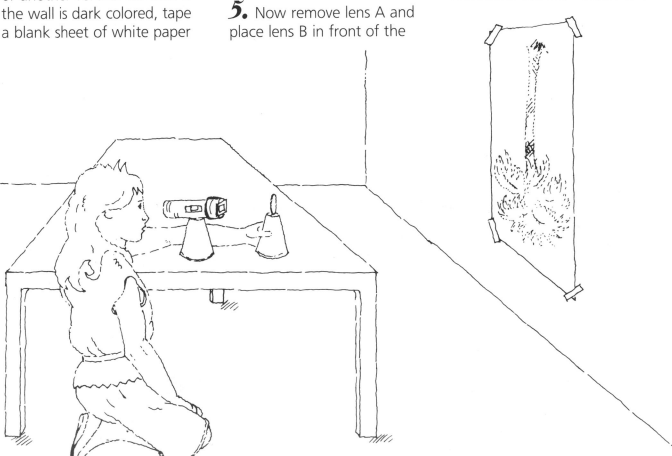

Behind the Scenes

Following is an overview of the major concepts addressed by the activities in this unit, plus further information for the teacher. The best way to understand how lenses work is to try out the activities on your own, and then to present them to your students. You will continue to learn more about lenses as you and your students gain hands-on experience, and, just like professional scientists, encounter new puzzles along the way.

If you choose to introduce some of the more detailed information provided in this section, do so only **after** your students have completed the activities. Do not read the text out loud to the class. Present the ideas in your own words, utilizing the drawings and analogies that you find most helpful in understanding what lenses do to light, and how they are used in magnifiers, cameras, telescopes, projectors, and the human eye.

What Lenses Do to Light

Light rays usually travel in straight lines, but it is not difficult to bend the rays. All you have to do is place a clear material (such as glass, plastic, or water) at an angle in front of the oncoming light. The greater the angle, the more the light will bend.

A jug or bottle of water illustrates this property. Place the jug in front of a picture or printed page. The picture or print will be stretched out sideways. To understand why this is so, imagine looking at the jug from above. A light ray that strikes the jug in the center goes right through without bending. But a light ray just to one side strikes the jug at a slight angle, so it is bent a little. A light ray striking the jug near its edge hits the edge at a steep angle. So it is bent a lot. The light rays are bent inwards, toward the center. This makes the rays appear as though they came from a much wider object.

The bending of light as it passes through a clear material is called *refraction*. Different kinds of glass, plastics, and other materials cause light to refract different amounts. For each kind of material, the amount of bending depends on the angle between the ray of light and the surface of the material. It is this interaction between light and transparent material that makes lenses possible.

Focal Length and Diameter

Unlike a jug, which is curved like a cylinder, most lenses are curved like a portion of a ball. One or both sides of a lens may be curved. The steeper the curve, the more the lens bends light. For example, look at the two lenses illustrated on this page.

Both lenses bend light from a distant object toward the axis of the lens, forming a cone of light. One lens is curved more steeply than the other, so it bends the light into a steeper cone. The point of the cone is called the *focal point*. The distance between the focal point and the axis of the lens is called the *focal length*. As you and your students will observe, lenses with a shorter focal length (more steeply curved) are more powerful magnifiers than lenses with a longer focal length.

The distance across a lens is its *diameter*. Lenses with a larger diameter collect more light, so they form brighter images in cameras and telescopes. Diameter and focal length are two of the most important properties of lenses.

Magnifiers

A magnifier works by "fooling" us into believing that the light comes from an object larger than the object at which we are looking. The person in the diagram is looking at the letter "B" printed on a page. Without the lens, the angle between the top and bottom of the letter would be very small. However, the lens bends the light that bounces off the letter (and surrounding paper) toward the axis of the lens. The letter now takes up a much larger angle, "fooling" the eye into seeing the object as much larger than it actually is!

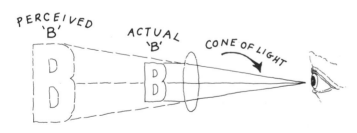

To be used as a magnifier, the lens must be close to the object—closer than the focal length of the lens. When the object is more than one focal length away, things appear smaller and upside down. As you look at a distant object with a lens in front of your eye, you can observe the "flip point" (or focal point) as you move the lens farther away, and the object appears to "flip" upside down. The reason why lenses turn images of distant objects upside down is explained in the next section.

Cameras

With a camera, if an object is very far away, like a distant mountain or the sun, the distance between the lens and the image is one focal length. But if the object is close—a few feet away—the image falls a little farther than one focal length away from the lens. That is why camera lenses must be *focused*, or moved a little bit farther away from the film, until the image is clear.

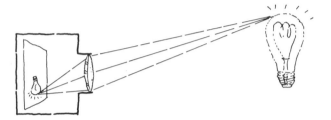

You may have noticed that some cameras have lenses that are very close to the film. These short focus lenses produce small images of objects, but show a wide area in the image. They are called *wide-angle lenses*. Most inexpensive cameras have wide-angle lenses. Very wide-angle lenses (called fish-eye lenses) encompass an extremely wide view. Cameras with lenses that stick out a long way from the film are long focus lenses. They make large images of objects, but pictures taken with them cover only a small area. They are called *telephoto lenses*.

The *f-number* of a camera lens is its focal length divided by its diameter. For example, a 50 mm diameter lens with a 100 mm focal length has an f-number of 100mm/50mm = 2. We say it is an f/2 lens. The *iris* in a camera allows you to reduce the usable diameter. This is called "stopping down" the lens. An f/2 lens can be stopped down to an f/4 lens by closing the iris until the diameter is just 25 mm. Reducing the f-number, or f-stop, cuts out rays from the edges of a lens that tend to be out of focus. If you have ever tried to read a distant sign by squinting, you have applied the same principle—reducing the diameter of the lens in your eye creates a more sharply focused image on your retina.

Telescopes

Telescopes use two lenses. One acts as a camera lens, and the other as a magnifier.

The front lens of a telescope is called the *objective lens*, because it is close to the object. Just like a camera lens, it produces an image of an object. If the lenses are not enclosed in a tube, you can hold a piece of paper at the focal point of the objective lens and see an image projected onto the paper. The image appears quite small.

The second lens is called an *eyepiece lens*, because it is close to the eye. It is used like a magnifier to make the image appear larger.

Like a camera, some telescopes have long focus objective lenses, and others have short focus objective lenses. Those with short focus objective lenses view a wide portion of the sky or landscape. They are called *wide field telescopes.* Those with long focus objective lenses make things appear very large, but show only a small portion of the sky or landscape. They are called *high power telescopes.*

The *magnifying power* of a telescope is defined as the number of times larger that an object appears when viewed through the telescope. Power may be determined by dividing the focal length of the objective lens by the focal length of the eyepiece. A telescope with a 500 mm focal length objective and a 25 mm focal length eyepiece has a power of 500mm/25 mm = 20 power, or 20x. You can increase the power of any telescope by using an eyepiece lens with a shorter focal length. Thus, if you replace the eyepiece lens with one that has a 10 mm focal length, the power of the telescope will be 500 mm/10mm = 50x. However powerful a telescope may be, the quality of the image depends mainly on the diameter and optical quality of the objective lens. Large diameter lenses allow a lot of light to enter the telescope, and make the image very bright. The power of a telescope to make faint objects brighter is called *light gathering power.* Some businesses that sell telescopes play up how much magnifying power a particular telescope has, but buyers should be aware that if the magnifying power is too high, the image quality and brightness will be so low as to render the telescope useless. In the case of astronomical telescopes especially, light gathering power and optical power are much more important than very high magnifying power.

Projectors

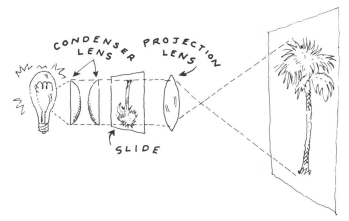

Slide projectors are very common in schools, and can be used to demonstrate some properties of lenses. A projector is like a camera in reverse. A camera forms a nearby image of an object that is a few feet to a few miles away. A projector forms a distant image of a slide that is very close to the lens. In this case, the slide is the object.

First, it is important to light up the object with very bright light, so when the light spreads out into a large image it can still be seen. This is done with a bright projection lamp. Two lenses located between this lamp and the slide concentrate parallel light rays on the slide. These are called *condenser lenses*.

The lens in front of the projector is called the *projection lens*. It can be focused (moved toward or away from the slide) until a sharp image is formed on the screen. If the screen is placed just a few feet away, the image will be relatively small and bright. If the screen is placed a longer distance away, it will be larger and dimmer.

Projection lenses may also be long or short focus lenses. Short focus lenses are used in small rooms where the screen cannot be too far away from the projector. They are called *short throw* lenses. Long focus lenses are used in large rooms where the projector must be a long way from the screen. They are called *long throw* lenses.

The Human Eye

We observe all the visual phenomena produced by magnifiers, telescopes, cameras, and projectors through lenses inside the human eye. Your students can gain a better understanding of how these internal lenses work after having experimented with the lenses used in these activities.

All of the light entering the eye must pass through the small black *pupil* in the center. The colored *iris* around the pupil automatically adjusts to limit or increase the amount of light that can enter. In bright sunlight, the iris contracts; when the light level is dim, the iris expands.

The pupil is protected by a thin, clear disc called the *cornea*. The lens is just inside the pupil. It projects images of everything we see, just as a camera lens does. However, there is an important difference between the way the lens of the eye focuses on objects at different distances, as compared to other optical devices. For example, in a camera the lens itself is moved closer or farther away from the film to focus the image, but in the eye, muscles attached to the lens change the curvature of the lens itself, thereby changing its focal length!

The back of the eye, called the *retina*, is covered with tiny sensors, shaped like rods and cones, that send signals to the brain when light falls on them. These signals are sent to the brain via the *optic nerve*. The signals include information on the brightness and color of the light.

Just as with a camera lens, the image formed on the retina of the eye is upside down. The brain turns the image right side up. A classic experiment explored this phenomenon. In the experiment, a person wore special glasses that turned the image on the retina right side up. For a while, the brain continued inverting the image, so the person actually saw things upside down. But after a few days, the brain adjusted to the new situation and turned the images around! (After the experiment, when the glasses were removed, the brain readjusted by going back to its usual function.)

Eyeglasses are needed when the eye lens no longer focuses images clearly on the retina. The lenses in eyeglasses are designed to change the steepness of the cone of light slightly, so it will focus more sharply. Eyeglasses for farsighted people converge the light, and eyeglasses for nearsighted people diverge the light, in both cases causing the eye lens to focus more clearly on the retina.

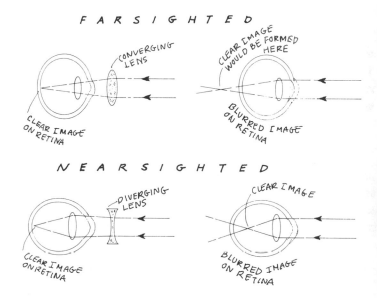

FARSIGHTED

CONVERGING LENS

CLEAR IMAGE WOULD BE FORMED HERE

CLEAR IMAGE ON RETINA

BLURRED IMAGE ON RETINA

NEARSIGHTED

DIVERGING LENS

CLEAR IMAGE

CLEAR IMAGE ON RETINA

BLURRED IMAGE ON RETINA

Glossary

camera—closed box with a lens and film for taking pictures.

diameter of a lens—the distance across a lens.

eyepiece—the lens in a telescope that is the closest to the eye; used mainly to magnify the image formed by the objective lens.

f-number—the ratio of the focal length of a camera divided by its diameter.

f-stop—the effective f-number of a lens when its diameter has been reduced, or stopped down.

focal length—the distance from the center of a lens to the focused image of an object infinitely far away.

focal point—the point where a focused image forms for an object infinitely far away.

focus—the condition of an image having clear and sharp edges.

image—a picture formed by a lens.

lens—a piece of glass, plastic, or other clear material that is curved so it will bend light.

light ray—a beam of light coming from a bright source.

magnifier—a lens used to make things appear larger.

objective lens—a lens at the end of a telescope that is close to the object. The objective lens forms an image of the object for magnification by the eyepiece.

power—the number of times an object is magnified.

projector—a box containing a lamp, condenser lenses, projector lens, and a place for holding a slide or film that is used to project a large image on a screen.

telescope—a combination of two lenses used to make distant objects appear to be closer.

Summary Outlines

Getting Ready Before the Unit Begins
1. Purchase lenses.
2. Mount lenses.
3. Duplicate data sheets.
3. Try out each activity yourself.
4. Read background information.
5. Arrange student work areas.

Getting Ready Before Activity 1
Fill jar with water.

Getting Ready Before Activities 2, 3, and 4
1. Prepare to darken room.
2. Set up lamp in middle of room.

Getting Ready Before Activity 4
1. Acquire flashlights and slides.
2. Prepare flashlights.

Activity 1: Magnifiers

Introducing Magnifiers
1. List things that use lenses.
2. Name four devices to be studied.
3. Define magnifier.
4. Ask questions about magnifiers.
5. Divide class into teams of three.
6. Distribute lenses and have students label.
7. Outline challenge: which lens makes things appear bigger?
8. Demonstrate how to use lenses.

Investigating Magnifiers
1. Go over data sheets.
2. Distribute data sheets.
3. Assist students as needed.
4. Collect lenses.

Discussing How Magnifiers Work

1. Ask which lens makes things appear larger.
2. Explain that the more curvature, the more magnification.
3. Demonstrate effect of jug of water.
4. Draw diagram of how a magnifier works.
5. Define magnifying power.
6. Students share their drawings of fingers.
7. Define field of view.
8. Students note view of faraway object is upside down.

Activity 2: Cameras

Introducing Cameras

1. Review.
2. Ask questions about cameras.
3. Distribute and explain data sheets.
4. Emphasize sharply focused image.
5. Tell students to notice whether bulb looks right side up or upside down.

Investigating Cameras

1. Distribute lenses.
2. **Remind students of their challenge: to measure the image distance of each lens.**
3. Turn on red light, turn off room lights.
4. Help students as needed.
5. Red light off, turn on room lights and collect lenses.

Discussing How Cameras Work

1. Ask for image distance measurements.
2. Define short and long focus lens.
3. Ask which lens projects a bigger image.
4. Draw diagrams to explain results.
5. Define telephoto and wide-angle lenses.
6. Ask why a real camera needs a box.
7. (*Optional*) Demonstrate camera.
8. Students share experiences with cameras.

Activity 3: Telescopes

Introducing Telescopes

1. Review.
2. Ask questions about telescopes.
3. Distribute and explain data sheets.

4. Outline challenge: which lens arrangement creates a telescope that makes things appear largest, and which creates a telescope with a wider field of view?

Investigating Telescope Lenses
1. Turn red lamp on, room lights out.
2. Distribute lenses and assist students as needed.
3. Remind students to switch lenses.
4. Turn out lamp, and turn on room lights.
5. Collect lenses.

Discussing How Telescopes Work
1. Ask which lens in front makes a more powerful telescope.
2. Ask which lens in front makes the widest field of view.
3. Draw diagram to explain telescope.
4. Ask if image was right side up or upside down. Ask why.
5. Have students look at eye pupils; telescope is light funnel.
6. Ask why a commercial telescope has tubes.
7. (*Optional*) Have students look through telescope.
8. Students share experiences with telescopes.
9. Explain binoculars.

Activity 4: Projectors

Introducing Projectors
1. Review.
2. Ask questions about projectors.
3. Distribute and explain data sheets.
4. Outline challenge: which lens will project a larger image of the slide?

Investigating Projectors Lenses
1. Distribute equipment.
2. Have students tape on slides. Assist as needed.
3. Turn red light on, other lights off.
4. Collect materials.

Discussing How Projectors Work
1. Ask which lens projects a larger image.
2. Draw diagram to explain projector.
3. (*Optional*) Demonstrate a commercial slide projector.
4. Define long- and short-throw lenses.
5. Ask general questions about lenses.
6. Students ask questions and share ideas.

MORE ON THEMES

The word "themes" is used in many different ways in both ordinary usage and in educational circles. In the GEMS series, themes are seen as key recurring ideas that cut across all the scientific disciplines. Themes are bigger than facts, concepts, or theories. They link various theories from many disciplines. They have also been described as "the sap that runs through the curriculum," to convey the sense that they permeate through and arise from the curriculum. By listing the themes that run through a particular GEMS unit on the title page, we hope to assist you in seeing where the unit fits into the "big picture" of science, and how the unit connects to other GEMS units. The theme "Patterns of Change," for example, suggests that the unit or some important part of it exemplifies larger scientific ideas about why, how, and in what ways change takes place, whether it be a chemical reaction or a caterpillar becoming a butterfly. GEMS has selected 10 major themes:

Systems & Interactions	**Scale**
Models & Simulations	**Structure**
Stability	**Energy**
Patterns of Change	**Matter**
Evolution	**Diversity & Unity**

If you are interested in thinking more about themes and the thematic approach to teaching and constructing curriculum, you may wish to obtain a copy of our handbook, *To Build A House: GEMS and the Thematic Approach to Teaching Science*. For more information and an order brochure, write or call GEMS, Lawrence Hall of Science, University of California, Berkeley, CA 94720. (415) 642-7771. **Thanks for your interest in GEMS!**

Name _____

Magnifiers

Hello

1. Use lens A to look at the writing in this circle. Now use lens B. Which lens makes the letters appear larger?

2. Use lens A to look at a part of your finger. Move the lens back and forth until your finger looks as large as possible and still is sharp and clear. Draw everything you see in the circle below.

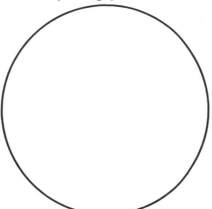

3. Use lens B to look at the same part of your finger. Move the lens back and forth until your finger looks as large as possible and still is sharp and clear. Draw everything you see in the circle below.

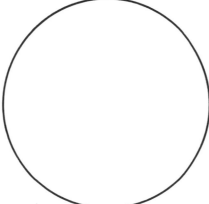

4. Hold either lens close to the writing on this page. Does the writing appear right side up, or upside down?

5. Look at something far away. Hold either lens in front of your eye and move the lens farther and farther until the object appears clear. Does it appear right side up, or upside down?

Cameras

Name _____

1. With the room lights off, place lens A on the table facing the lamp. Fold a blank sheet of paper so it will stand up. Place the sheet of paper behind the lens and move it back and forth until you see a picture of the lamp on the paper. This picture is called an *image.* Move the paper back and forth carefully until the image is sharp and clear.

2. With the ruler on this page, measure the distance between the center of the lens and the sharp, clear image on the paper. This distance is called the *image distance.*

3. What is the image distance of Lens A? _____

4. What is the image distance of Lens B? _____

5. If you replace the sheet of paper with film and surround the lens and file with a box, you have a camera. If you want a camera that makes large images, would you use a lens with a long image distance or a short image distance? _____

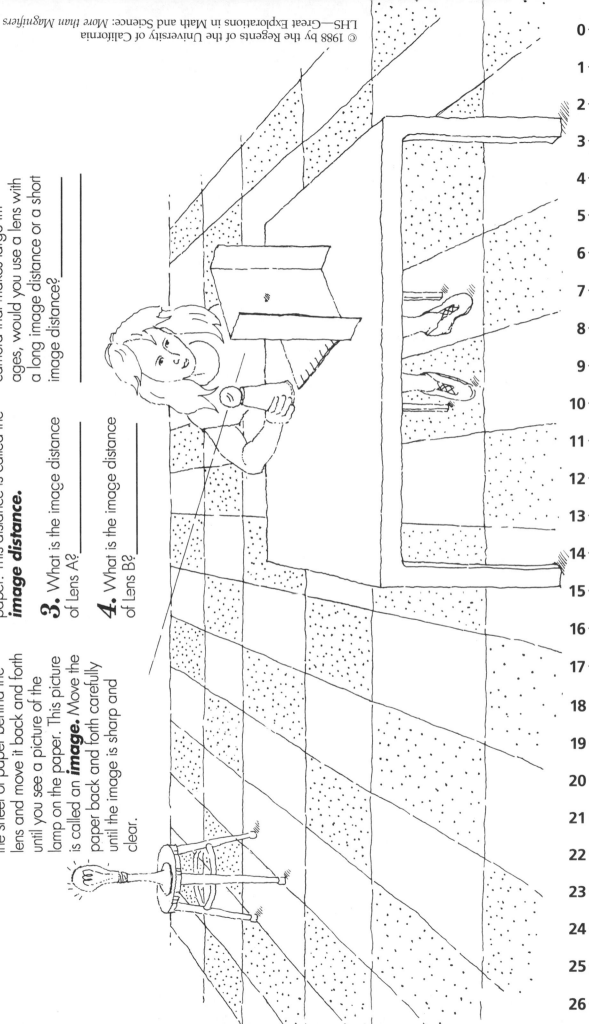

0
1
2
3
4
5
6
7
8
9
10
11
12
13
14
15
16
17
18
19
20
21
22
23
24
25
26

Telescopes

Name _____

1. Use lens A (short focus lens) to make an image of the light bulb on a sheet of paper. Place lens B (long focus lens) behind the paper and use it as a magnifier to look at the image.

2. While you are looking at the image through lens B, remove the paper. You will see a "telescopic view" of the light bulb!

3. Now do the same procedure, but use lens B to make the image, and have lens A next to your eye, to magnify the image.

4. The lens in front, that is used to make the image, is called the **objective** lens because it is closest to the object you are viewing. The lens closest to your eye is called the **eyepiece.** Both lenses together are called a **telescope.**

5. If you want a telescope that makes things look as large as possible, which lens would you use for the objective lens, a short focus or long focus lens? _____

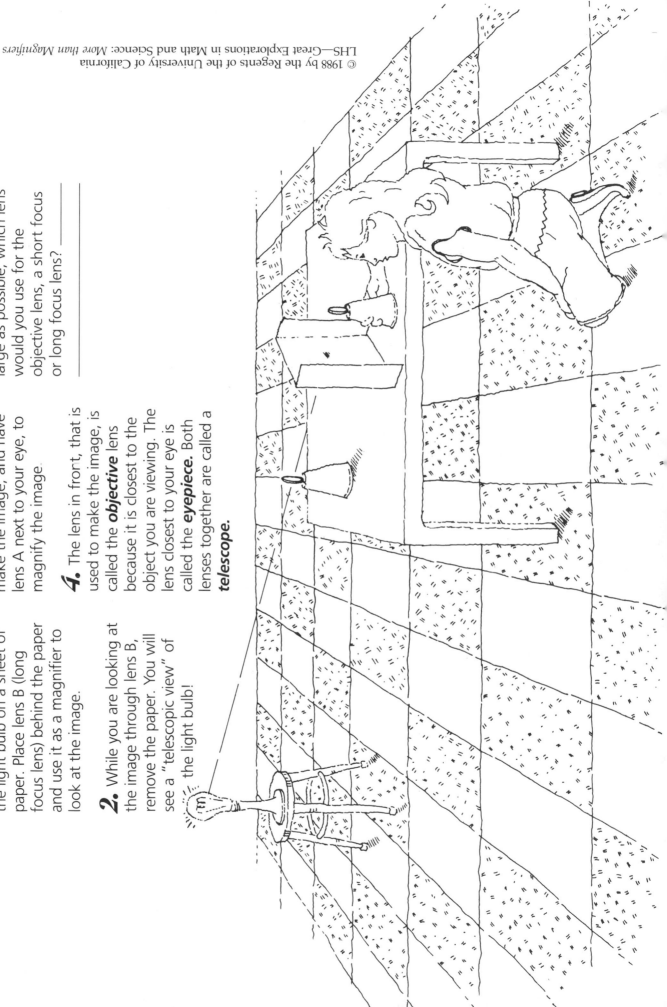

Name _____

Projectors

In order to make a table-top slide projector that makes as large an image as possible, which lens would you use, a long focus or short focus lens? Follow these steps to find out!

1. Tape the flashlight to the bottom of a cup, making sure that you can turn it on or off.

2. Turn the slide upside down, and tape it to the end of the flashlight.

3. Position the flashlight on a table or desk, about 1.5 meters away from the wall or another vertical surface. If the wall is dark colored, tape a blank sheet of white paper to the wall, at the same height as the flashlight.

4. Point the flashlight with slide attached toward the wall. Place lens A in front of the slide. Slowly move the lens away from the slide and toward the wall until you see a sharply focused image of the slide projected onto the wall.

5. Now remove lens A and place lens B in front of the slide. You will have to move the lens quite a distance toward the wall before it will focus. If you cannot focus an image at all, move the flashlight with slide further from the wall and try again.

6. Which lens projects a larger image, the long focus lens or the short focus lens?

_____

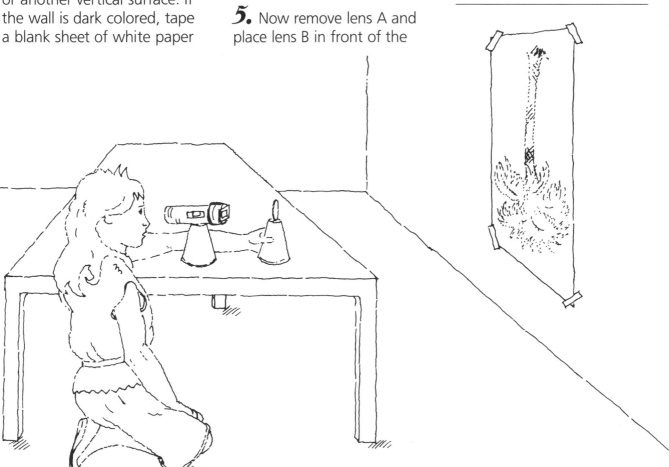

© 1988 by the Regents of the University of California
LHS—Great Explorations in Math and Science: *More than Magnifiers*

GEMS Guides

TEACHER'S GUIDES

Acid Rain
  Grades 6–10
Animal Defenses
  Preschool–K
Animals in Action
  Grades 5–9
Bubble-ology
  Grades 5–9
Buzzing a Hive
  Preschool–3
Chemical Reactions
  Grades 6–10
Color Analyzers
  Grades 5–8
Convection: A Current Event
  Grades 6–9
Crime Lab Chemistry
  Grades 4–8
Discovering Density
  Grades 6–10
Earth, Moon & Stars
  Grades 5–9
Earthworms
  Grades 6–10
Experimenting with Model Rockets
  Grades 6–10
Fingerprinting
  Grades 4–8
Global Warming
  Grades 7–10
Height-O-Meters
  Grades 6–10
Hide a Butterfly
  Preschool–3
Hot Water & Warm Homes from Sunlight
  Grades 4–8
Involving Dissolving
  Grades 1–3
Liquid Explorations
  Grades K–3

Mapping Animal Movements
  Grades 5–9
Mapping Fish Habitats
  Grades 6–10
More Than Magnifiers
  Grades 6–9
Of Cabbages & Chemistry
  Grades 4–8
Oobleck: What Do Scientists Do?
  Grades 4–8
Paper Towel Testing
  Grades 5–8
QUADICE
  Grades 4–8
River Cutters
  Grades 6–9
Vitamin C Testing
  Grades 4–8

ASSEMBLY PRESENTER'S GUIDES

The "Magic" of Electricity
  Grades 3–6
Solids, Liquids, and Gases
  Grades 3–6

EXHIBIT GUIDES

Shapes, Loops & Images
  all ages
The Wizard's Lab
  all ages

SUPPLEMENTARY MATERIALS

GEMS Teacher's Handbook
GEMS Leader's Handbook
A Parent's Guide to GEMS
To Build a House: GEMS &
  the Thematic Approach to
  Teaching Science

● *Please contact the GEMS project for a descriptive brochure and ordering information.*

Write or call
GEMS
Lawrence Hall of Science
University of California at Berkeley 94720
(415) 642-7771